M000013692

FREEWRITING FOR TRAVEL WRITERS

HOW TO USE A CREATIVE FREEWRITING TECHNIQUE TO IMPROVE YOUR TRAVEL WRITING

JAY ARTALE

BIRDS OF A FEATHER PRESS

For Information contact:

www.birdsofafeatherpress.com

Cover and Interior Design by **Birds of a Feather Press**

First Edition: January 2017

ISBN Print Version: 978-1-944370-01-5

My Favorite Quote:

"We don't stop playing because we grow old; we grow old because we stop playing." - George Bernard Shaw

CONTENTS

PART ONE

INTRODUCTION TO FREEWRITING

As travel writers we need to continually strive to create engaging content, and this book shows you how to use freewriting to elevate your travel writing from one-dimensional to attention-grabbing.

CHAPTER ONE

WHAT IS FREEWRITING?

In this concise how-to guide, you'll learn everything you need to know to start your freewriting journey.

OPEN THE CREATIVE FLOODGATES

Freewriting is a technique writers use to tap into their creative side. It can be used to overcome writer's block, or a warm-up exercise to get your writing muscles working.

The goal is to fill the page with words that flow from you like a stream of consciousness. You do this by relaxing your conscious mind so that your subconscious mind takes over.

LIBERATE YOUR WRITER'S VOICE

Freewriting allows you to access a stream of creativity that lies just below the surface of your consciousness. Train your mind to access those thoughts, and you will release your inner creative writer.

The most challenging aspect of freewriting is to break the bad habits that interfere with your ability to channel those subconscious thoughts. It's about tuning out your conscious thoughts, and tuning into the subconscious ones.

MASTER THAT LITTLE VOICE IN YOUR HEAD

We all have a little voice in our heads that criticizes and comments on everything we do, see, and hear. Rather than using that little voice to correct spelling or grammar, or criticize your writing as you write, surrender to it. Tap into your subconscious and capture what your little voice is saying.

The more you free write the easier it becomes. Stick with it and you'll reap the benefits. Most writers need to practice freewriting multiple times before it feels natural and effective. So be patient.

TRANSITION FROM ANALYTICAL TO CREATIVE

Freewriting will help you move from conscious (deliberate) writing to subconscious (automatic) writing. When you achieve success, your words will stream from you without consciously thinking about them.

If you're usually an analytical thinker, freewriting may sound a little "out there", and to be honest that was my initial impression. But once you've used the freewriting technique a few times you will start to feel more attuned to your creative side. So, don't knock this creative process until you've tried it!

～

WHAT'S WAITING FOR YOU INSIDE?

PART ONE covers how nonfiction writers can use this creative writing technique to improve their travel writing. We take a brief look of how your pyramid of thoughts works and the benefits of using freewriting. We detail out seven of the core travel writing challenges, and provide solutions for dealing with them.

PART TWO provides an easy to follow step-by-step approach for planning and conducting your freewriting sessions.

PART THREE features two examples of my freewriting sessions and an evaluation of the output. I show you how productive freewriting is for generating article ideas.

PART FOUR is a resource section with a 100 freewriting prompts to trigger your creative thought process. Plus my top three travel writing tips, and a couple of resource lists.

CHAPTER TWO

FREEWRITING PIONEERS

We live in a world of ads, fads and consumer culture. You can't browse the internet today without being pitched a *"brilliant new technique"* designed to help you achieve your writing goals. If you're skeptical about the benefits of freewriting you should consider its history.

It's not a new concept. Teachers and writing experts have been advocating the freewriting technique for decades. Dorothea Brande, a teacher, led the way for a succession of writers and academics to refine the freewriting concepts she brought to the forefront.

∼

In 1934 Dorothea Brande wrote "Becoming a Writer". It's a writer's classic that covers writing and the creative process. This was decades before brain research delved into the role of the right and left brain. Dorothea taught her students how to still their minds and call forth their inner writer. In her book she advises readers to sit and write for 30 minutes every morning, as fast as they can.

> For decades popular culture has touted that logical, methodical and analytical people are left-brain dominant, while creative and artistic types are right-brain dominant. The myth has since been debunked. Scientists did a series of tests that showed participants used their entire brain equally throughout the course of the experiments, rather than using different brain hemispheres for analytical vs. creative tasks.

Source: Live Science

In the mid-seventies, Peter Elbow advanced freewriting in his book "Writing Without Teachers". He advocated non-stop or free uncensored writing, without editorial checkpoints, followed by the editorial process at a later stage. His approach was aimed at writers who get stuck or blocked.

In 1986 Natalie Goldberg released her first book about for writers "Writing Down the Bones: Freeing the Writer Within" which brought together Zen meditation and writing in a new way. Her First Thoughts approach involved keeping your hand moving and not crossing out. The goal is to just get your words onto the paper.

Probably the most well-known book that incorporates freewriting is "The Artist's Way: A Spiritual Path to Higher Creativity" by Julia Cameron, which was first published in 1992, and a 25th Anniversary edition is now being sold.

~

Author Mark Levy taught writing at Rutgers University, and in 2010 published "Accidental Genius: Using Writing to Generate Your Best Ideas, Insight, and Content". He used freewriting for years to solve all types of business problems and to generate ideas for books, articles, and blog posts.

~

I'm showcasing these freewriting advocates for two reasons:

1. As an example of how this successful writing technique has endured for nearly 100 years, and
2. To provide you with an opportunity to investigate the topic in more detail.

~

CHAPTER THREE

CAN NONFICTION WRITERS USE FREEWRITING?

Although freewriting is used extensively by fiction writers, it's also an extremely useful tool for nonfiction writers.

No matter what type of writer you are, sometimes you're going to to struggle with how to start a new chapter of your book, or get in the right head-space to write your next blog article.

Freewriting helps you brush away the analytical cobwebs and forces your mind to rely more heavily on your creative side.

WHY I USE FREEWRITING AS A PRE-WRITING TECHNIQUE

Writing travel guides and nonfiction books is a methodical and analytical exercise. There's a lot of research and fact-checking to be done, and then there's the structural organization of the content. All of these activities rely on systematic thinking. But your words also need to leap off the page to connect with your audience. In order to achieve this you need to create content that evokes an emotional reaction in your reader.

It is all too easy to get stuck in an educational or informational rut when writing nonfiction. As soon as you tap into the inspirational side of a topic you create content that is multi-dimensional.

MY INTRODUCTION TO FREEWRITING

I was first introduced to this technique during a writer's class I regularly attend when I'm in Turkey. During the sessions we use writing prompts and 20-minute freewriting bursts to create creative narratives. I'm a nonfiction author and initially I kept my freewriting activities firmly ring-fenced within my creative writing classes.

During these sessions I was able to write more prolifically and I learnt how to use freewriting to overcome writer's block. It also forced me to connect more closely with the prompt topics, so that my writing had more depth.

It didn't take me long to realize how beneficial it would be to apply this successful writing technique to my nonfiction activities. So now I use freewriting to approach the seven different travel writing challenges I face.

This book explains the basics of freewriting and how you can use this writing technique to overcome the writing challenges you encounter.

CHAPTER FOUR

YOUR PYRAMID OF THOUGHTS

Throughout this book I mention the conscious and subconscious mind. So this brief introduction explains how your conscious, subconscious, and unconscious thoughts flow.

Think of these three areas of your mind working together like a pyramid.

Your conscious mind is at the top, your subconscious is in the middle, and your unconscious mind is the foundational layer at the bottom.

Let's take a look at each one individually:

1. YOUR CONSCIOUS MIND

When you're in the present moment your awareness is leveraging your conscious mind. Your conscious mind is aware of external surroundings and some internal mental functions.

2. YOUR SUBCONSCIOUS MIND

Your subconscious mind, also known as your preconscious mind, consists of accessible information. This is where your recent memories live.

When you direct your conscious mind to your subconscious you can access stored information.

That is the crux of freewriting.

Your subconscious is also the conduit that allows uncon-scious thoughts to bubble up to your conscious mind.

3. YOUR UNCONSCIOUS MIND

Your instinctual drive and the information you can't access directly from your conscious mind lives in your unconscious.

During your early years you acquire countless memories and experiences that have created who you are today.

You can't recall most of these early memories because you've either repressed them or forgotten them. But the beliefs, habits, and patterns you established as a child are there in your unconscious mind, and they are what drive your adult behaviors.

In summary:

- Freewriting brings subconscious and unconscious thoughts into your conscious mind, so that you can capture them on paper.
- Your conscious mind can't access your unconscious thoughts directly, so it needs to use your subconscious as a conduit.

CHAPTER FIVE

WHEN TO USE FREEWRITING

MORNING, NOON OR NIGHT

Use the freewriting technique whenever you need it. Start your day with a session to get your writing muscles warmed up. Freewrite throughout the day to energize your writing. Or end your day with a freewriting session to capture your dormant thoughts.

Freewriting allows you to subconsciously explore a train of thought. It takes you in a direction your conscious mind hasn't dared venture into.

Some of your thoughts will lead you to a dead end, but others may spark an idea that is well worth expanding into a fully fledged article.

Here are three scenarios where freewriting can play an active role:

AS A WARM-UP EXERCISE:

All forms of physical activity requires some kind of warm-up, and writing is no different. Freewriting is a pre-writing technique that gets your writing muscles warmed up.

AS A PRE-WRITING TECHNIQUE:

Freewriting allows you to subconsciously explore a train of thought. It takes you in a direction your conscious mind might not have dared to venture. Some of your thoughts will lead to a dead end, but others will trigger an idea that you can expand into a fully fledged article. When you use freewriting as a pre-writing technique, you create a plethora of ideas to pull from before you start writing your writing assignment.

TO INCREASE CREATIVITY:

The act of timed non-stop writing forces your mind to form new ideas. When you start capturing these on paper, your creative juices allow your ideas to flow. This stream of ideas will move you through any writing challenge you face.

Your creativity kicks into overdrive to come up with new ideas and areas to explore.

∾

CHAPTER SIX

SEVEN TRAVEL WRITING CHALLENGES

It's so easy to get stuck in a rut when you're writing travel articles. If you're not connecting emotionally with your topic it is too easy to rely on using cliches, or sharing a generic experience that is similar to every other traveler's experience.

But when you use freewriting to tap into your subconscious you strip away that primary analytical layer and tap into the emotional core of how a destination or experience made you feel.

Whether your reader is an armchair traveler or somebody planning their own trip, your job as a travel writer is to inspire them. You need to transport them to their destination and leave them satisfied that their lives have been enriched by your experience. You can't achieve this if you're simply relying on recounting facts and figures. Get to the heart of a destination by tapping into your senses, making the story personal, and being specific.

You can also use freewriting as as warm-up, pre-writing,

or idea-generation exercise to increase the effectiveness of your travel writing sessions.

I've outlined seven different ways you can use freewriting to overcome the challenges we face as travel writers:

1. **Power through writer's block**
2. **Get out of a travel writing rut**
3. **Solve a writing problem**
4. **Leverage for productive procrastination**
5. **Overcome boredom**
6. **Use as a confidence booster**
7. **Create a fun distraction**

Let's look at the following challenges in more detail:

1. POWER THROUGH WRITER'S BLOCK

One of the primary reasons to freewrite is to overcome your writer's block. If you don't know how to approach a specific topic, freewriting can trigger a stream of ideas to get you started. This is especially useful when you're searching for a different angle or tone for a new travel writing assignment.

When you use brainstorming to generate a list of ideas, this relies on using your conscious mind. But when you switch to freewriting you tap into your subconscious mind. This deeper approach generates inspiring ideas that will get your creative juices flowing.

 I've often said that there's no such thing as writer's block; the problem is idea block.

JEFFERY DEAVER, CRIME WRITER

One of the biggest writing challenges is coming up with new and original content every time. Freewriting will generate a whole range of different thought directions. You will amaze yourself with the level of creativity and the sheer volume of ideas you generate.

Whenever you encounter writer's block, freewriting will help you blast right though that feeling of being stuck. It opens up new possibilities and concepts, and lets your thoughts and ideas flow.

2. GET OUT OF A WRITING RUT

Have you fallen into a rut of regurgitated ideas? Freewriting can jolt you out of it by generating ideas or different ways to approach your topic. When familiarity breeds contempt, shake it off by tapping into your creative side.

 There's a very fine line between a groove and a rut.

CHRISTINE LAVIN, SINGER SONGWRITER

Freewriting can help you tap into your subconscious to see where your words lead you. It's all about putting the logical side of your thought process on hold and surrendering to your creative side.

I usually straddle the fence between analytical and creative. So I use freewriting to force myself out of my methodical and analytical thinking and surrender to a creative flow.

3. SOLVE A PROBLEM

Freewriting can help you generate solutions to any writing problem you're currently wrestling with. Your subconscious can help you create ideas that are not immediately visible. It helps you discover different and more creative ways to approach your current writing dilemma.

This problem solving approach is an opportunity to use Blue Sky thinking.

(Blue Sky: original or creative thinking, unfettered by convention and not grounded in reality.)

 If you change the way you look at things, the things you look at change.

WAYNE DYER, AUTHOR & PUBLIC SPEAKER

Potential solutions will stream through the floodgates providing you with plenty of inspiration to draw from. Some ideas will be unrealistic, but they could end up being the first step to a feasible solution.

And an additional benefit? Freewriting can help you vent your frustrations and change your perspective.

4. LEVERAGE FOR PRODUCTIVE PROCRASTINATION

Have you ever jumped onto social media and wasted an hour achieving next to nothing because you're scrolling through social media posts and comments, telling yourself you'll watch just one more video and you'll get to writing?

 Imagination only comes when you privilege

the subconscious, when you make delay and procrastination work for you.

HILARY MANTEL TWO-TIME WINNER OF
THE MAN BOOKER PRIZE

Instead of wasting time on social media, you can set yourself a freewriting session that will help you warm up your writing muscles and get you inspired and invigorated to write what you need to write.

5. OVERCOME BOREDOM

No matter how much you love writing, sometimes the thought of writing a blog post or another chapter for your book can feel uninspiring.

 Running through things because you are familiar with them, breeds routine and this is the seed of boredom.

SIR JAMES GALLWAY, FLUTIST

It's easy to get bored with doing the same writing tasks over and over again if that's all you do. So freewriting is a good opportunity to mix up your writing assignment.

It's like stopping your marathon runs and opting instead for a sprint. This change in routine is all you need to lull your body and mind out of being bored. When you mix things up, you keep your writing fresh.

6. USE AS A CONFIDENCE BOOSTER

There are times when you will doubt your writing ability.

> Self-doubt is real. Everyone has it. Having confidence and losing confidence is real, too, and everyone has been in that position.

VENUS WILLIAMS, TENNIS CHAMPION

This usually happens to me when I read an amazing bit of travel writing that I'd wish I'd written. So when confidence in my own writing abilities is waning I use freewriting to tap into my creative side. Each time I've done this, I've been amazed by the level of creativity and sheer volume of ideas I'm able to create when I push myself. A successful freewriting session is a powerful motivator.

7. CREATE A FUN DISTRACTION

Writing can sometimes feel like a chore. Especially when you have multiple assignments to deliver or a word-count target to hit. Use freewriting as a fun exercise to write for the pure joy of the process of creating, rather than to achieve a specific writing goal or word-count objective.

≈

Freewriting is one of the most useful tools for generating ideas, getting unstuck, or increasing your levels of creativity. Even if you set yourself a short freewriting session, your mind will start thinking in new and exciting ways.

≈

PART TWO

FREEWRITING, STEP-BY-STEP

The key to freewriting is to do it fast and within a specific timeframe. Start by engaging your creative side and writing until the timer stops. Here's your seven-point plan for achieving a successful freewriting session:

1. **Create you ideal writing conditions**
2. **Set a deadline**
3. **Determine your freewriting goal**
4. **Choose your freewriting prompt**
5. **Relax your conscious mind**
6. **Don't stop - keep moving**
7. **Don't edit or censor yourself**

Let's look at each of these in more detail.

CHAPTER ONE

STEP 1: CREATE YOUR IDEAL WRITING CONDITIONS

I provide a step-by-step freewriting approach that everyone can follow, but this initial step is something you must decide for yourself. Only you know what your ideal writing conditions are.

WHAT ENVIRONMENT WORKS FOR YOU?

Do you shut yourself away in a quiet room with no distractions to write successfully? Or do you prefer music or the buzz of chatter in the background to get your creative juices going?

Freewriting is an individual and personal process. If you're not sure what your ideal writing conditions are, try different environments.

My Preference? Silence.

WHAT TOOLS WORKS FOR YOU?

My husband would attest that I have a mouse and keyboard permanently attached! But there are specific occasions when I rely on a notebook and pen to capture my words - and freewriting is one of them.

There's something visceral about that connection between your brain, arm, hand, and pen working in unison to create you words on a page.

But the primary reason I rely on paper and pen is to avoid the habit of hitting the backspace key to delete what I don't like. I also find it too easy to get distracted by reading what's on my screen.

My Preference? A5 notepad, and a felt-tip or fountain pen.

Experiment with your environment and tools to create the ideal writing conditions to get the most out of your freewriting session.

 There is no right or wrong way, it's what's right for you.

～

CHAPTER TWO

STEP 2: SET A DEADLINE

Set a deadline so that there's a sense of urgency to write as fast as you can, but don't rush. Freewriting should be approached as an enjoyable sprint. When your timer starts, go full speed ahead until the timer stops.

Even if you can't think of what to write you still need to scribble as fast as you can, even if it's just writing "I can't think what to write, I can't think what to …." etc. Eventually your creative side will kick-in and take over again.

POMODORO TECHNIQUE:

I use the Pomodoro Technique for my freewriting sessions.

Basically all activity takes place in 25-minute bursts and then you take a 5 minute break and start another 25-minute burst of activity.

An hour's worth of freewriting should be all you need to overcome your writer's block or create the creative breakthrough you're looking for.

If you're just freewriting for a fun distraction, one shorter session may be all you need.

There's no hard and fast rules about the ideal length of freewriting session. At the end of the day it's personal choice. I've found that the Pomodoro Technique works for me, but if you feel a 25-minute session is too long you can adjust it.

A freewriting session needs to be long enough to allow you to tap into your creative side and stop you from relying on your regular (conscious) thought-pattern.

Another option is to use two freewriting sessions to approach an idea. Use your first 25-minute session to just clear the cobwebs out of the way, and rather than trying to tweak and polish this freewriting output, take a 5-minute break and do another freewriting session using the same prompt.

OTHER TIMEFRAMES:

I'd recommend freewriting for at least 10-minutes per session. But you could also play around with 15 or 20-minutes sessions and see how productive they are for you.

I actually use 20-minute sessions to write first drafts of my poetry. This is because it's the time limit that's dictated by the group facilitator, but it works well for getting concepts and ideas onto a page.

At the other end of the spectrum, your session can last as long as you can maintain creative thought. But it's tiring and you'll soon discover what your upper limit is.

The more you practice freewriting the easier it becomes. You should discover that new ideas pop into the forefront more quickly each time you practice.

≈

CHAPTER THREE

STEP 3: DETERMINE YOUR FREEWRITING GOAL

I find it easier to get into the freewriting zone when I know what I'm trying to achieve. So I always determine why I'm freewriting, before I start.

You can pick from any of the seven challenges I detailed in the previous chapter to set your intention.

Here's the list as a reminder:

1. Power through writer's block
2. Get out of a writing rut
3. Solve a problem
4. Productive procrastination
5. Overcome boredom
6. Use as a confidence booster
7. Create a fun distraction

∾

CHAPTER FOUR

STEP 4: CHOOSE YOUR WRITING PROMPT

Always write your freewriting prompt at the top of the page so it's a reminder of what your subconscious mind is tapping into.

This prompt can be the topics you want to generate ideas for, or the problem you're trying to solve.

If you're freewriting as a warm-up exercise or as a fun distraction I've included 100 freewriting prompts later on in the book to pull from. Alternatively, you can create your own prompt.

COLLECTING AND SAVING PROMPTS:

I use Evernote to organise all my notes and inspiration for freewriting topics. I stumble across these prompts when I'm on social media or browsing websites. But I also get inspired by what I see around me each day.

No matter where I find potential prompts, I can easily save

them, take a photo of them, or record them into my phone or computer. I tag them as "Writing Prompts" so they're easy to locate as a later date.

You can even go old-school and capture your prompts in a notebook. (Let's face it; we always have one of two of those lying around!)

Always be on the lookout for inspiration so that when you sit down to freewrite, you always have a ready supply of available prompts at your fingertips.

HOW TO REUSE A PROMPT TO SOLVE A PROBLEM:

To solve a problem using freewriting, pose the questions you need answered and then set your timer and start capturing your thoughts about the problem.

Use one whole session to capture all of your thoughts about the problem, and don't even get to the solution.

Then schedule another freewriting session to capture the solutions.

HOW TO REFINE A PROMPT TO BUILD ON AN IDEA:

Later in the book I show you how I used two freewriting sessions to build on creative ideas.

In my first session I set the following prompt:

- How do I create a niche approach for writing about Paris?

In my second session I set myself a prompt to investigate a theme (Spring) that kept popping up in my first session:

- Paris in the Springtime

You can keep doing freewriting sessions to delve deeper and deeper into a topic each time.

~

CHAPTER FIVE

STEP 5: RELAX YOUR CONSCIOUS MIND

Of all the freewriting steps, this is the most difficult. It will take practice and patience to master.

Each time you wrangle your conscious mind to relax you'll find it easier to access your subconscious thoughts.

BE POSITIVE:

It shouldn't come as any surprise that positive thoughts have the power to lift your spirits. A whole field of research has sprung up around Positive Psychology; those who are more grateful than bitter, are more positive.

Positive thoughts affect your heart's rhythm and your body's nervous system. This triggers a change in your emotional state, and your ability to dig deeper for creative inspiration.

It's a three-step process:

1. Mediate about what you're grateful.

2. Clear away the clutter and doubts swimming around your conscious mind.
3. Access your subconscious.

Whole books and careers are built around how to meditate. I can't do the topic justice in this guide, but do want to introduce you to mindful meditation.

Becoming mindful relies on your ability to be aware of yourself and your breathing.

Start practicing with 5-minutes of mindful meditation to help get you in the creative zone. If you've practiced yoga before this technique should be familiar.

Mindfulness Preparation:

- Find a room or space with the least amount of distractions.
- Get comfy on the ground or in a chair.
- Set your timer for the 5-minutes.

Focus on your breath:

- Don't do the shallow breathing you do throughout the day (in your chest), take deep breaths and feel it in your stomach.
- Your breath will start to slow as your breathing becomes more deliberate and you become more aware of it.
- Concentrate on that split second between the end of one breath and the beginning of a new one.

- After you've exhaled completely, take a mindful pause, before inhaling a new breath.

Surrender your mind:

During your mindfulness meditation you will have thoughts swirling around your brain. Don't try and block or stop these thoughts. It will just frustrate you.

Instead, wrap your thoughts up in each exhale. Focus back on your breath, and how your body feels as you breathe in and out.

Simple, yes?

If you struggle to do this mindful meditation technique by yourself, you can easily find a practitioner to lead you through a session.

Search on YouTube for Mindful Meditation for Beginners and there are plenty of 5-minute videos to lead you through it. I won't recommend one specifically because what appeals to me may not appeal to you.

∾

CHAPTER SIX

STEP 6: DON'T STOP - KEEP MOVING

Don't stop. Don't pause.

Just keep writing until the timer stops.

The majority of my creative writing is done via a keyboard, so I prefer freewriting using a notebook and pen. I find it easier to keep my hand moving with a pen in my hand, and I like the physical connection between hands, pen, and words on a page.

 As the rhythm of a train can rock you to sleep, the rhythm of your writing can lull your conscious mind into silence. Staying in motion creates a physical momentum that releases you from your habits of judging your writing and your ideas, thus giving you access to the raw, buried treasures of your mind.

SAGE COHEN, AUTHOR OF THE POETIC LIFE

Whichever writing method you prefer you just have to keep your hand moving, because when you stop that's when your critical eye starts taking over.

∾

CHAPTER SEVEN

STEP 7: DON'T EDIT OR CENSOR YOURSELF

When I write an article it's easy to get stuck on a specific sentence and to rework it again and again because the word-choice, punctuation or grammar isn't quite right. But with freewriting, you need to get rid of all of those editing hurdles and just let the words flow.

Even if what you're writing doesn't make any sense. Your goal is to fill your blank page with your words, and block your inner-critic.

Don't question what you're writing. Just believe in the creative process and keep going.

If you're freewriting is a throwaway exercise, you don't have to go through the editing process. But if you actually want to use it as an idea generator, you can spend time tweaking and polishing it to make it ready for prime-time.

∾

These seven steps are all you need to develop your own freewriting experience.

1. **Create you ideal writing conditions**
2. **Set a deadline**
3. **Determine your freewriting goal**
4. **Choose your freewriting prompt**
5. **Relax your conscious mind**
6. **Don't stop - keep moving**
7. **Don't edit or censor yourself**

CHAPTER EIGHT

RECYCLE YOUR FREEWRITING

In my 25-minute freewriting sessions I usually generate about a thousand words. Some of the content is unusable, but there will always be a couple of golden nuggets that are worth mining. These aren't always relevant for the current task or assignment, but may work as inspiration for something in the future.

Always keep your freewriting for reference so you can come back and review for inspiration at a later date.

If you spot some potential ideas in your freewriting output, you can highlight them so that you can spot them more easily when you come back to the idea-well.

∾

PART THREE

MY FREEWRITING EXAMPLE

In the following freewriting example I set myself 25-minutes to freewrite about "**How do I create a niche approach for writing about Paris?**" I've included my unedited output in this chapter. (I did this exercise on my laptop to capture the content, but I usually freewrite using a paper and pen).

The text is unedited and includes typos and grammatical errors, but I did **bold** three segments after I'd finished the session for illustrative purposes. These three bold segments make the least amount of sense in the whole piece, and are where my creative flow was interrupted. Rather than just stopping and staring at a blank page, I wrote whatever words popped into my head. Before too long the words started flowing again.

∾

CHAPTER ONE

FREEWRITING SESSION #1

Time: 25 minutes

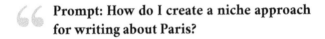 **Prompt: How do I create a niche approach for writing about Paris?**

(Spelling mistakes and grammar issues are intentional)

∽

What do I like about Paris? What would other people like? What is new? What is old. Do I want to tap into something that is going to have mass appeal or do I want something quirky. I need to identify a target audience and appeal to them. Do I consider the weather. I like the idea of Spring. What topics or things appeal in spring. I could use that spring is the start of something, things are blooming. What about flowers. Are there national flowers of paris. What about using flowers and the history if impressionistic painting. Is there something that would bind the season to something paris is used for, and somebody that paris is famous for to create a thread that would keep the article on topic but that covers people, places, things. Is there a colour that could be the thread. What smells are lingering in the air. I think of bread and croissants and coffee. Standing at the coffee counter in an expresso bar, eating a crispy croissant as opposed to standing in line at a Starbucks and ordering an Americano. People watching. Dogs shitting on the sidewalk. Things that you don't expect in Paris. What to avoid. **Things. Flowers. Spring. Cold. Sights and sounds. Elephants the size of big houses. What can you pack in your trunk. What to take to paris and what you leave behind.** Historical markets of paris. What attitude you need to bring with you when you come to the city. Where to meet the people you can interact with. What do you like doing yourself, how to get around. What thread ties activities and passions. Can you paint a picture yourself, are there places you can do a painting class, what about a cooking class. Are the movies that you can use to tie into session you are here. Recreating movie events by using them as inspiration for a trip to Paris. Fashion. Design your own outfit. Where to wear it. **The colours of spring kids avoiding the masses quiet places to sit and think. Places to draw.** Where did the famous artists eat and drink. Drawing where they drew. In the Monmatre areas where you can walk down the cobbled streets. I visited Van Gogh's neighbourhood and there's the windmill that is iconic. Is it red. And they are used to mill flower, and iconic food is croissant so what is the lifecycle of a croissant. Eat it draw it? Thinking. Big cushions. Degas and his ballerinas. Lots of traffic. Cycling. Spring. Red windmill. Walking. A walking tour of eating and an activity. A weekend in paris for him and for her. With one itenerary for a man and one for a woman. Is this sexist? Maybe have itinearies but dont' tag them as gender specific. Experience something, create it yourself and then eat and drink in the neighbourhood that is iconic or tied to it. Where are croissants made. Is there a bakery that will give you a lesson in how to make a croissant. Start your day eating a croissant and drinking an expresso, and then visit a street market that has food vendors, and then go to a cafe where the impressionist painters used to eat and drink, and then visit a museum to experience their art, and the use the images in their art to create a walking tour. So you're seeing the city through their eyes in the paintings and then walking through the part of the city that was the inspiration for the art. Or pick one picture and create a walking tour from that painting. Using sights, sounds, smells the painting evokes to create a physical experience. What do people expect when they come to paris. Good fashion. Good food. Cutlure. Walking. What about those paninis they sell on the street. The streets are where it's happening. Outside vs inside. Eating on the street. Street art. Famous street artists. How street artists are inspired by great historical artists. Art lessons. Article aimed at creatives. Where to go to write or draw. How to get inspired, and where to go to create your own works of art. Art could be writing, painting, or a dish, or a drink. Icnonic cocktail of paris. Experience and see. Walk and contemplate. Do and recreate. Get something out of the city of give something back. How to get involved. Local community. Get underneath the skin of the city. Take it in from a fresh pair of eyes. Can we really visit an old iconic city like paris and shine a new light on it and see it from a new perspective. Do we need to look at it as an old city, or do we need to look at it as an ever changing animal that is aways being redeveloped. What is new. This is old is new again. Cycles of trends and activities. Cycle of art trends. The old masters the impressionists and the street artists.

How fashion and art appear in every day. Seeing paris through new eyes. A fresh new look. **Spring. Tulips roses horses carts dying cemeteries who is buried there, why did they die their.** Famous people who have made paris their home. Why did they move there. What is the draw of paris. City of love but love of what. Couples. They music in the music halls. Concerts. Sounds in the streets. Modern art and modern music is changing the city we don't know why this is true. Does the city need something. Is it missing something. Do visitors still feel enamoured with the city after they leave. A dog lovers city.

∾

CHAPTER TWO

SESSION #1 EVALUATION

Let's take a closer look at the first bold segments where my flow was interrupted:

Things. Flowers. Spring. Cold. Sights and sounds. Elephants the size of big houses. What can you pack in your trunk. What to take to Paris and what you leave behind.

• "Things" is a filler word I used to keep my hands moving.

• Then I started haltingly to capture elements triggered by Spring (*Flowers, Spring, Cold*)

• After my series of single word ideas, I forced out the three-word idea of "Sights and Sounds". Again it's another series of filler words.

• This led to a bizarre sentence about elephants the size of houses. This is where my subconscious started to kick in again.

• Then it wrote a word association between elephants and with what can you pack in your trunk.

• Then these thoughts of elephants and their trunks triggered a thought about what you take to Paris and what you leave behind. This is where my creative flow started again.

Both of the other bold segments are equal gibberish, but each of them triggered a creative stream of ideas that could be potential article ideas.

> *The colors of spring kids avoiding the masses quiet places to sit and think. Places to draw.*

> *Spring. Tulips roses horses carts dying cemeteries who is buried there, why did they die their.*

In both of these cases by just powering through the creative block, I was able to get back on track to generate more ideas.

This "sticking with the flow until it triggers an idea" is true each time I got stuck.

I use freewriting exercises a lot, so I only got stuck three times in this 25-minute session. Don't worry if you get stuck more frequently. What's important is that you power-on through these flow-blocks and just write random words or sentences. They don't have to make sense when you write them, as their role it to trigger a stream of creativity.

It was interesting to me that each time I got stuck, a Spring-theme popped up in the filler words, and also in other parts of the writing. I don't know why this subconscious-theme popped up or where the fascination with this season in Paris came from, but when themes happen in your freewriting they make good fodder for further evaluation.

You could even do another freewriting exercise using the theme in your writing to develop the idea further, like I did in the following exercise.

~

CHAPTER THREE

FREEWRITING SESSION #2

Time: 25 minutes

 Prompt: Paris in the Springtime

(Spelling mistakes and grammar issues are intentional)

∿

Paris is known for fashion so in spring people still need to wear their coats. When is paris fashion week. Wat events go in during this time. What are the famous fashion icons that could feature as the central part of an article. Where did they live what era. Could they bring a new perspective on an old city. Breaks Water river eating swans birds feathers indians immigrants in Paris. The impact of immi-grant in the fashion culture of paris. Would paris be what it is today without immingrants. Famous exports from france what do they drink. I there a famous drink. Absinthe. Van Gogh. Are the gardens that are best only seen in spring, what flowers are most prevalent in spring. Would a colour themed article be intersting, or would it be too stages. Spring means new beginnings. The start of new potential. Yellow purple white gold amber blue flag colours of the flag when does the colour of the flat mean. Leaving the city to go to that palace Let them eat Cake. Marie Antoinette. Versaise From Versaise to Versace But he's Italian. So who is a famous parisienne fashion designer. The undiscovered belly of the fashion district. Paris fashion on a budget. Shopping guide to paris in the spring. Markets second hand clothese. Is paris the city for old clothes of is that a fashion faux pas. Will there be fashion for dogs. What do dogs where in springs. Why do the french love their dogs so much? If the cow bull never do if be then see tulips smell sweet smell of the bakeries where to get breakfast in paris before you walk around the public parks. Are their boat trips along the seine that you can hop from garden to garden. Can you only look at flowers or are there other things to do at these gardens. What else is new this time of year? Beaujolias Neauveax. What wine. What about champagne, is there a time of year for new vintages. Can you take a day trip out of paris to do champage tasting. Where is the champagne tasting region. Are there wine shops in paris. New wine new cheese crusty bread A cheese lovers guide to paris, wine and cheese afternoons in the city of love. Red wine, red cheese. What about the colours of the flag. White red and blue. White bread white garlic, red wine and blue cheese. These things are good for you. French love fashion they love to eat and then when they eat they drink and they laugh and they play music. What events only happen in spring. tie the red white and blue into the season's events. What other elements of the city would fit into this red white and blue, could you incorproate something educational or is that too non-holiday. Who it make sense to write for women on a girls trip … spa weekends in paris with champagne breaks and red white and blue in the afternoon. Coffee tips and chocolate. How to indulge without the bulge win paris. What to do when you're feeling blue? Can you enjoy paris on your own. Where can you go on your own without feelign lonely, where can you visit with ease, can women go to a cafe and sit and people watch and not be bothered. Whould you want to go to paris and do that? Would you like to go to paris? I'd be happy to go on my own and then what would I do .. An art tour and eveyone needs to eat. So waht other elements would fit into my red white blue theme… are oywsters typical of paris .. What about croque madam and croque mousieur … could I use those two typical french dishes to create an article .. Paris from both sides of the street. Men and women. Mild bread wild bread. Mild wine, strong wine. Mild cheese strong cheese. The mild and wild sides of the paris street. High art low art. High fashion low fashion. Series of article from two completely different perspectives. No middle ground just extremes. Just put the high fashion, high cost elemtns out there as something to aspire too, and then for people ofn a budget, what is possible … graphitti street art the art of the streets a tour of where it can be seen. Is it legal? Bring then if to see then water boats food big posh rstaurant using our red white blue theme and street markets what about food trucks are they prevalent in paris … a food truck tour and markets. The epicenter of events the epicentre of where to walk where to ride, what to see what to taste. People with taste and people without taste. The freaks of paris. Why spring brings out the freaky side of paris. How can you fit right in if you've never been before the basics of not creating a scene. Or causing a faux par. The faux side of paris. Big expensive and the copy cats. The artistis the facihsion desingners what do they all bring to the city. Does the city owe any of them anything. What doe paris own you. What shoudl you exxpect. Can you expect your visit to be fulfilling if you're only there a day. What day is pbest to go. Hump day in the city of love … all events on Paris on a wednesday .. Are there things that are only available to do, see on a wednesday. What about hump back bridges over the river or over the road. What other hump things are there? Is tehre food that could be associated with hump? When I think of hump what do I think of see when is the life and times of a famous painter.

～

As you can see, my "Paris in the Springtime" prompt ended up being a a catalyst for getting my creative juices flowing. The rest of my freewriting session went off in many different directions, It wasn't long before the Spring theme was no longer a pivotal train of thought.

That's the beauty of freewriting; you never know where it will lead you.

～

CHAPTER FOUR

ARTICLE IDEAS FROM MY SESSION

I spent 50-minutes freewriting about Paris and ended up with a variety of potential article topics.

Here's just 10 ideas that jumped out at me, and I know I could double this list if I spent more time delving into the content:

1. **"See and Draw Paris: A walking tour for Artists"** with a resource section of art shops for buying supplies. *(So many visitors go to Paris to tour galleries, museums, and view the art. Many of them are artists themselves, and this article would tap into that niche).*

2. **"The Ultimate Croissant: 1-day cooking classes in Paris".** *(Two iconic aromas of Paris for me are strong espresso and warm buttery croissants. They trigger an emotional reaction, so the goal of this article would be to tie the fact-based list of cooking classes with the emotional connection of these two Parisienne favorites).*

3. **"A glimpse of Art in Paris: From Impressionism to Street Art"** *(On my last trip to Paris I took lots of*

photos of eye-catching street art but didn't do anything with them. So this is an example where memories of these photos were triggered to the forefront via freewriting).

4. **"Fashion Conscious Paris on a Budget: The City's best thrift stores"** (*This article could be timed to coincide with Paris Fashion Week*).

5. **"Day Trips from Paris for a sip of Champagne"** (*I Googled this topic and you can reach the champagne region from Paris by train in an hour*).

6. **"Alone in Paris? Fall in love with the city"** (*Tips about solo activities travelers can do in this city that is synonymous with couples and love*).

7. **"The Mild and Wild sides of your Paris Table"** (*A food-themed article about comparisons, e.g. the best strong and mild cheeses of Paris, or the best bold and light red wines. Locations of cafes that offer wine and cheese tasting, or restaurants that offer cheese and wine pairing lessons*).

8. **"Gastronomic Paris: And the Food Truck Revolution"** (*Paris is synonymous with fine-dining, so I'm intrigued by the idea of delving into a food truck article*).

9. I like the two potential titles: **"The Freaky Side of Paris"** and **"Hump Day in the City of Love"**. (*I'm not sure what these articles would focus on, but if I decided to pursue these ideas I'd do a freewriting session to trigger some ideas worth researching*).

10. **"Get Real in Faux Paris"** (*I Googled "Faux Paris" and discovered that the French built a second version of Paris on the outskirts of the city. This was done at the end of the First World War to fool the Germans. I'm intrigued to find out more Faux-related topics - and this historical discovery would be a good basis for an article*).

≈

So there you have it. 50-minutes of freewriting created ten solid article ideas worth investigating.

What's more, these thoughts originated from my subconscious and unconscious so I have an emotional connection them. This connection will help to elevate the quality of my travel writing. It will bring the content alive by making it personal.

This is the key to taking your travel writing from one-dimensional to attention-grabbing.

≈

There are literally millions of travel blogs on the internet. So, is it too late to develop your own travel writing activities into an online brand? *Hell No!*

Some bloggers are here today and gone tomorrow. Others like Nomadic Matt, Adventurous Kate, The Expert Vagabond (another Matt), yTravel (Caz and Craig), theplantetD (Dave and Deb), and The Blond Abroad (Kiersten) are continuously in the top echelons of the travel blog community.

Competition is fierce. There's a continual stream of travel blogs sprouting up each day, and hoards of existing travel bloggers jostling for position in the search results.

If you don't develop a niche or travel speciality to focus on, you run the risk of getting lost in the shuffle.

 I think the most important thing is to have a well-developed voice and personality along with a few specialties on which you can become an expert.

> I recommend being as narrow and focused in your topic(s) as possible.

> Your niche should be what made you fall in love with travel in the first place. Was it food, adventure, luxury, romance? The possibilities are endless. But most of all, it should be your personality.

I'm a firm believer in the value and benefits of establishing a content niche. That's exactly how I started my first travel blog back in 2012, and I have used the same approach for my latest website I launched in 2016.

For my **Bodrum Peninsula Travel Guide** website I focus on one specific area of Turkey, and I write for independent travelers who want to get off the beaten path and connect with the local community.

For my **Birds of a Feather Indie Author Press** I focus on travel writing, and target bloggers who want to self-publish their own travel guides and nonfiction books.

But a specific niche is not enough to hang you travel blogger hat on.

What can elevate you head and shoulders above many of the travel bloggers out there is quality content.

If you use **freewriting** to tap into your **creative well of inspiration** you will have a personal connection to your topic.

This will not only improve the quality of your travel writing, but it will help you build an avid following.

～

PART FOUR

RESOURCES

CHAPTER ONE

100 FREEWRITING PROMPTS FOR TRAVEL WRITERS

I've put together this list of a hundred travel writing prompts to inspire your next freewriting session:

1. The lights flickering on the water bring up so many old memories, like the time...
2. Dancing on the Cantina patio was exhilarating, making me forget entirely about...
3. I don't know why I brought her on this trip, but seeing her reaction to this stunning sight made me...
4. I'm standing on top of a the City's biggest skyscraper, a breeze is wafting through my hair, I look down and see...
5. My pack is too heavy and my back aches, so it's about time I...
6. It's dark and there's a hissing sound coming from outside our hut, so I stand up to investigate and discover that...
7. Walking through the dense rainforest, moisture trickles down the back of my neck and...

8. I'm walking aimlessly through the city streets and suddenly hear…

9. While writing a postcard my pen runs out of ink, and am devastated that I didn't get to write that…

10. Looking back through the travel photos I took during the day, my favorite one shows…

11. I was so psyched to go on today's hike, but it didn't meet expectations because I really wanted to…

12. After a grueling eighteen hours I finally reached my destination, but when I arrived…

13. Hungry from the long journey, my first stop is a local market, where I…

14. After an exhausting climb I finally reach the lookout pointe - it's breathtaking but…

15. I quickly look behind me and see…

16. The old cathedral walls drip with history. My skin prickles with the anticipation of…

17. This bitter wind whipping across my face makes me wish…

18. When the stepping stones are this far apart, I'm liable too…

19. I looked into his eyes and felt…

20. If that bridge swings about this much in the driving rain, I'm…

21. Last time I was here, I wish I'd…

22. There are three things that I really like about…

23. I can't still taste the most memorable meal I ate in…

24. This is the reason I like this part of the journey is…

25. As I sit here, stuck at the traffic lights in this packed bus, my mind wanders to…

26. If it hadn't have been for that group, I would never have….

27. I shouldn't have waited so long to…

28. I wiped the sweat from my brow, and then laid…
29. How can something this ugly, taste so…
30. I take one more look at my map, and then head…
31. Is it too early to…
32. Those unspoken words she conveyed with her eyes made me…
33. When dawn rises in this part of the country, it reminds me of…
34. I'll never forget that travel blogger in…
35. If only I'd reached forward and…
36. I'm holding a hard hat, waiting to tour the site, but my fingers are trembling because…
37. The zip-line started to pick up speed, but the only thought that crossed my mind was…
38. I reluctantly took a sip. Their eyes gazed at me expectantly, so I smiled and said…
39. The train carriage lurched back and forth. I would have fallen, if it hadn't been for…
40. The long pink tendrils trailed across the path. I jumped over them to reach…
41. The smell of dusty books in this old shop really makes me wish…
42. I was so thirsty, I think I was even willing to drink…
43. The heat from the hot air balloon almost singed my eyebrows, so next time…
44. The seats were comfy. What is that delicious aroma I can smell?..
45. Another day on the road without…
46. I rummaged around in my bag, and was thankful I'd finally laid my hands on…
47. It's not often I say this, but…
48. It's at times like these that I wonder about my

decision to lead the type of lifestyle I fought so hard for.

49. This is a great pitch I've written, it really depicts…

50. If I don't hear back from that editor this week, I'm going to…

51. I rubbed the dirt off the window, and enough light came in so that I could…

52. I'm so pleased I remembered to pack…

53. If I hadn't been travelling on that day, I would never have had the opportunity to meet…

54. As I was racing forward to catch my next ride, my foot slipped…

55. I couldn't decipher the noise coming from the bush. When I edged closer I was relieved to see…

56. I don't mind getting wet when I travel, but the one thing I really enjoy is…

57. Before I forget, let me tell you about…

58. If it hadn't been for this one travel memory, the whole trip would have been…

59. The anticipation is building. I'm so looking forward to bringing…

60. My itinerary wouldn't be complete without a…

61. That parting gesture will always cause a lump in my throat because…

62. I really shouldn't have bought that last…

63. For me, what makes a trip really memorable is when…

64. How fortunate that I got to experience…

65. Thank goodness I was kept in the loop about…

66. What a trip! These high and low points will stick with me, and…

67. Their parting words filled me with anticipation during the entire…

68. Each time I hear that song it will always remind me of...
69. We didn't have language in common, so instead we...
70. In the background, I heard...
71. I'm so pleased I brought this particular book along with me...
72. I wished I'd experienced...
73. It's fortunate that I got to hear...
74. This newsworthy event rocked the locals, but I just couldn't...
75. Could this weather make me feel any more...
76. They use that word a lot, but to me it feels...
77. They called it mysterious, but what they really meant...
78. Coming back home after a long trip always makes me...
79. It's a mundane task, but I relish it because I always know that...
80. If I had to summarize key points from my last trip it would have to include...
81. Just as they waved goodby, my friend reminded me...
82. I wish I'd experienced this country from the perspective of...
83. I thought this stereotype didn't exist anymore until I visited...
84. For some reason, this part of a trip always feels more like a chore because...
85. My view of the world has changed since experiencing...
86. Who could have imagined that friendship could blossom between...
87. If I could interview them again, I would ask...

88. At the time I couldn't see it from their point of view, but now that...

89. I was so relieved that I was the one getting on the plane to travel...

90. This is the last person that I wanted to share a cabin with, but by the end of the journey...

91. If I could just live just one day in their shoes I would...

92. I wish I could close my eyes and suddenly be transported to...

93. It's my first trip on this subway and it surprised me because...

94. When I think of visiting here again, I don't know if...

95. This souvenir will always remind me of the time I...

96. I wasn't sure if they understood, but when they smiled and...

97. If it wasn't for that last glass of water...

98. I'm so grateful that I stopped to...

99. When the agonies of that trip fade, I'm still going to remember the girl who...

100. If only...

～

CHAPTER TWO

TOP 3 TRAVEL WRITING TIPS

In order to help your audience connect with your writing you have to help place them into the scene you're creating with your words.

1. USE YOUR 5 SENSES

All too often travel writers fall back into the easy chair of recounting what we see and overlook the other 4 senses. Don't forget to share the smells, sounds, tastes, and touch sensations of your travel experience.

Most readers want to read travel articles for planning purposes or escapism. They don't want to have to work too hard when they read your narratives. They want to feel the atmosphere of the location you write about, without stumbling over tired clichés or overused words.

When these clichés or words creep into your stories, it's time to find new ways to describe your scenes with your other senses.

2. TAP INTO YOUR EMOTIONS

Convey whether your travel experience triggers terror, pure joy, a sense of achievement, elation or just boredom, and those feeling will be at the heart of your travel writing.

3. BE SPECIFIC

The name of somebody you encountered, or the name of the street you lost your red purse are extra details that add an element of authenticity to what you're writing.

Another way to be specific is to avoid flat adjectives and generalizations. Rather than calling a view spectacular, describe what you're experiencing and let the reader draw their own conclusions that what you're describing is indeed spectacular. (Show Don't Tell).

∾

Obviously travel writing is a lot more involved than these three points, but if you get these three elements right the quality of your travel writing will shine through.

∾

CHAPTER THREE

FREEWRITING RESOURCE LIST

Here's some additional articles that feature the hows and whys of freewriting:

The Book Designer:

https://www.thebookdesigner.com/2010/04/unleash-your-creativity-now-how-to-freewrite/

The Writers Digest:

http://www.writersdigest.com/tip-of-the-day/freewriting-discover-your-inner-voice-find-inspiration-to-write

AIMS University:

http://www.aims.edu/student/online-writing-lab/process/freewriting

Easy Way To Write:

http://easywaytowrite.com/Free_Writing.html

Writing Forward:

https://www.writingforward.com/creative-writing/writing-practices-free-writing

Copy Blogger:

http://www.copyblogger.com/free-writing/

Orna Ross

http://www.ornaross.com/benefits-f-r-e-e-writing/

If you have discovered a useful freewriting article that has helped your creative writing, please email me so that I can update this resource list.

email: jayartale@gmail.com

≈

DOWNLOAD A SET OF FREEWRITING WORKBOOKS

I've created a set of freewriting workbooks using the prompts in this book. Send me an email to and I'll send you the link to download them for free.

≈

CHAPTER FOUR

WRITING RESOURCE LIST

Here's my primary writing resources:

EVERNOTE

The be all and end all of note taking and capturing snippets from the internet. I love that I can forward an email to my Evernote account so that it doesn't get lost in my inbox. I use Evernote Premium, which allows me to search within PDFs.

- More Information: https://evernote.com/

SCRIVENER

A productive creative writing program. There's a slight learning curve on this software, but once you have it mastered there's no looking back.

- More Information:
  https://www.literatureandlatte.com/

VELLUM

Simple and effective ebook formatting. Vellum makes it easy to format your own ebooks, and if formatting isn't your thing, I offer an inexpensive ebook formatting service via my Birds of a Feather Press.

- More Information: https://vellum.pub/

CANVA

I'd be lost without the creative freedom of using Canva to create my web, social and book images.

- More Information: http://www.canva.com

TOGGL

I use the free version of this time-tracking software. It's an efficient way to track how you're using your time, and really helps to estimate how long it takes you to complete a specific task. I also use it to time my freewriting sessions.

- More Information: http://www.toggl.com

ASANA

For task management and project planning I use Asana. I'm part of multiple Asana teams. On my own account I use the free version, but I'm part of a couple of premium teams that are hosted by freelance clients.

- More Information: https://asana.com/

TRELLO

Another task management program that I use primarily as a guest blog tracking tool. I capture guest blog leads and then track my communication with the blog hosts.

- More Information: http://www.trello.com

HEMINGWAY

I use the free online version of the Hemingway App to improve my writing. It helps me identify passive or difficult to read sentences so that I can make my writing more approachable to a wider audience.

- More Information:
  http://www.hemingwayapp.com/

STRONG VPN

For security purposes I use a VPN service when logging onto public WiFi, and my VPN provider of choice is Strong VPN.

- More Information: http://www.strongvpn.com/

~

EPILOGUE

I love the sense of ownership and simplicity that self-publishing provides. After twenty years in a corporate job I finally followed my dreams to become a self-published full-time writer. This book is just one more example of how I'm thriving and surviving.

 Don't leave your dreams on the shelf too long. Grab them by the reigns and ride them long and hard towards to horizon.

JAY ARTALE

~

 Originally from the flatlands and big skies of rural Norfolk in eastern England, Jay lived in the States for two decades before relocating to Turkey.

> *"When we got married we had a 5 year plan to press the reset button to move to greener pastures - but life had other ideas. This 5 year plan became a 10 year plan, and then as we were approaching a 15 year plan ... I realized that the life we were living wasn't a dress rehearsal, so action was needed."*

After 17 years in Los Angeles working as a Project Manager for a global entertainment company, she took a long-awaited life diversion. She coupled her move to Turkey, with the launch of her writer career.

Jay launched and manages multiple successful blogs, and has published travel guides and nonfiction books.

She also helps companies establish and build an online presence with social media and content marketing.

BLOGS & WEBSITES

- www.rovingjay.com (Roving Jay: Nomadic Adventures in Wonderland)
- www.birdsofafeatherpress.com (Indie Author Press for Travel Writers)
- www.bodrumpeninsulatravelguide.co.uk (Bodrum Peninsula Travel Guide website)

SOCIAL MEDIA

- Jay Artale on Twitter: @jayartle
- Jay Artale on Pinterest: @jayartle
- Bodrum Peninsula Travel Guide on Facebook: @BodrumPTG

ASSOCIATIONS

Jay is a member of the following organizations:

The Alliance of Independent Authors

ALLi, the Alliance of Independent Authors, is a non-profit association for writers who self-publish.

International Travel Writers Alliance

The world's largest association of professional travel journalists.

≈

Contact Jay via email:
jayartale@gmail.com

CURRENTLY AVAILABLE

- Bodrum Peninsula Travel Guide: Turkey's Aegean Delight
- Gumusluk Travel Guide: Bodrum's Silver Lining
- Turkey Tales: A Bodrum Travel Memoir in Verse

TRAVEL GUIDES - IN THE WORKS

- Exploring Bodrum: Day Trips in Turkey's Basement

TRAVEL MEMOIR - IN THE WORKS

- Sugar Cubes Under a Mavi Sky

HOW TO GUIDES - IN THE WORKS

- Guest Blogging for Travel Writers: How to Build your Author Brand by Sharing your Travel Passions and Expertise
- Pinterest for Authors: How to Build your Author Brand with Pins and Boards
- An Introvert's Guide to Building your Brand from your Subject Matter Expertise using eBooks

- How to Write a Travel Guide: Book 1 "Plan it"
- How to Write a Travel Guide: Book 2 "Pen it"
- How to Write a Travel Guide: Book 3 "Produce it"
- How to Write a Travel Guide: Book "Promote it"

∼

Visit the Birds of a Feather Press website to see our Production Schedule:

www.birdsofafeatherpress.com/books/

∼

YOUR OPINION COUNTS

I hope you have enjoyed: **Freewriting for Travel Writers**

Other readers use reviews to help them make their purchasing decisions, so please take a few minutes to leave a review for my book at your favourite online retailer or Goodreads.

Thanks! Jay